THE LONGEST SHOT

HOW LARRY KWONG CHANGED THE FACE OF HOCKEY

CHAD SOON AND
GEORGE CHIANG

illustrated by
AMY QI

ORCA BOOK PUBLISHERS

To Zoe, for giving me a chance. To my children,
Quinn and Jasmine, and to every kid with a dream—
I'm cheering for you to give it your best shot. —C.S.

To my son, Lee, for the fond hockey memories we share. —G.C.

Text copyright © Chad Soon and George Chiang 2024
Illustrations copyright © Amy Qi 2024

Published in Canada and the United States in 2024 by Orca Book Publishers
orcabook.com

Library and Archives Canada Cataloguing in Publication
Title: The longest shot : how Larry Kwong changed the face of hockey /
Chad Soon with George Chiang; illustrations by Amy Qi.
Names: Soon, Chad, author. | Chiang, George (Actor), author. | Qi, Amy, illustrator.
Description: Includes bibliographical references and index.
Identifiers: Canadiana (print) 20230219632 | Canadiana (ebook) 20230219640 |
ISBN 9781459835030 (hardcover) | ISBN 9781459835047 (PDF) | ISBN 9781459835054 (EPUB)
Subjects: LCSH: Kwong, Larry, 1923-2018—Juvenile literature. | LCSH: Hockey players—Canada—
Biography—Juvenile literature. | CSH: Chinese Canadian hockey players—Juvenile literature. |
LCGFT: Biographies.
Classification: LCC GV848.5.K86 S66 2024 | DDC j796.962092—dc23

Library of Congress Control Number: 2023936366

Summary: This illustrated nonfiction book for middle-grade readers tells the story of
how Larry Kwong became the first player of Asian descent in the NHL.

Orca Book Publishers is committed to reducing the consumption of nonrenewable resources in the
production of our books. We make every effort to use materials that support a sustainable future.

Orca Book Publishers gratefully acknowledges the support for its publishing programs provided by
the following agencies: the Government of Canada, the Canada Council for the Arts and the Province
of British Columbia through the BC Arts Council and the Book Publishing Tax Credit.

Cover and interior artwork by Amy Qi
Design by Troy Cunningham
Edited by Kirstie Hudson

Printed and bound in South Korea.

27   26   25   24   •   1   2   3   4

Contents

PREFACE

When I was a kid in the 1980s, my grandfather George Soon told me about one of his heroes, a Chinese Canadian hockey player named Larry Kwong, who was a star of the 1940s and '50s. I read every hockey book and magazine I could find, but not even one mentioned Kwong's name. Decades later, a newspaper article by journalist Tom Hawthorn reminded me of that mysterious name from the past. In 2007 there was little else about Larry Kwong on the internet. So I phoned the then 84-year-old man himself. I thanked Larry for inspiring my grandpa. I asked him to share his story with me. He graciously did, over countless hours, during weekly calls and on many visits, for more than 10 years until his death in 2018.

I miss Larry, my hero and friend. The story of his life never ceases to amaze me. I hope you feel the same.

—Chad Soon

One

HUMBLE BEGINNINGS

LARRY'S HOMETOWN IN THE 1920s

Nestled between three lakes at the head of the Okanagan Valley, the Vernon of Larry Kwong's youth was a picturesque town of 5,000 people. Orchards, farms and pastures spread from the valley floor up the rolling hills and mountains. Just south of the main-street shops was Chinatown, where the Kwongs lived above their general store. About 500 Chinese Canadians called the modest buildings on the neighborhood's three streets home. Boarding houses were packed with Chinese farm workers. Some ran small businesses like restaurants and laundries, which attracted white customers to Chinatown. Many other white residents wanted the Chinese community gone.

ANTI-ASIAN HATE

The idea that Chinese were filthy, diseased and drug-addicted was commonplace in North America at that time. Racist *stereotypes* caused fear of and hate toward Chinese immigrants and their families. People also accused them of stealing jobs from white workers. In 1907 an anti-Asian rally in Vancouver drew thousands of people and turned into a riot. The mob attacked Vancouver's Chinatown and Japantown, smashing windows and terrorizing residents. In Vernon, the Kwongs hoped that their neighborhood would be spared a similar fate.

KWONG HING LUNG

Larry's father, Ng Shu Kwong, came to Canada from China in 1882. He opened his store in Vernon's Chinatown in 1895. Kwong Hing Lung (which means "abundant prosperity") was a "Canadian" shop with something for everyone, from tea and silks to macaroni and cowboy hats. The store brought in a diverse crowd, including Chinese, Japanese, white and Indigenous customers. Around town people began to call Larry's father Kwong, after the name of his store. "Our real family name is Eng," said Larry, "but

CHINESE HEAD TAX

As the Canadian Pacific Railway was nearing completion in 1885, thanks in large part to Chinese workers, the prime minister, John A. Macdonald, turned around and slapped a hefty tax of $50 on any Chinese person entering the country. The tax was later raised to $100, then to $500.

as the store my dad had was called Kwong's, we decided to adopt that as the family name."

TWO MOTHERS

Business was good, and in 1904 Ng Shu Kwong arranged to bring a second wife, Loo Ying Tow, to Canada. He paid the Chinese head tax, which by then had risen to $500, or about two years' worth of wages for an immigrant worker. Mr. Kwong already had two children with his wife Rose. At that time, it was considered acceptable in Chinese culture to have more than one wife. As the second wife, Loo Ying Tow was expected to take over most of the housework. Rose, or First Mother, would have six children in total. Loo Ying Tow gave birth to nine more, including Larry. He was born in Vernon on June 17, 1923, the 14th of 15 siblings and the youngest son. Larry was given the Chinese name Eng Kai Geong.

HUMILIATION DAY — JULY 1, 1923

When Larry was only two weeks old, the Canadian government scrapped the head tax and passed a new ***Chinese Immigration Act***. No more Chinese people, with very few exceptions, would be allowed to come into the country at any price. So while most Canadians celebrated the country's birthday on July 1, there was a day of mourning in Canada's Chinatowns. There it became known as Humiliation Day. Under this racist law, also known as the Chinese Exclusion Act, families like the Kwongs were separated. Larry's sister-in-law Sue was ***deported***. To be with his wife, Larry's oldest brother, Harry, had to move to China.

GREAT LOSS

When Larry was five, his father became sick. "He had to stay in the parlor because it was the quietest room," said Larry. On January 13, 1929, Ng Shu Kwong died of cancer. Before the funeral procession, Larry's mother tied a white mourning band around his head and told him not to look back as they were walking, as that was bad luck. "I remember walking quite a ways to the cemetery," said Larry. "Finally I was picked up by a family friend, trudging through snow. The town's marching band was out." Later that year the **Great Depression** hit the Kwongs' family business hard—they had to scrape by.

FIRST GRADE

In September 1929 Larry started first grade at South Vernon Elementary. School was a big adjustment for Larry. He was used to the people and language of Chinatown, and he knew only a little bit of English. He felt out of place. "For me, in those days, Canadian meant white people," explained Larry. He felt lucky to

find two friends in George and Edgar Dobie. Their family ran the Vernon Hotel. Larry's sister Betty said the trio was inseparable and always easy to spot because they were "two redheads and one black head." The Dobie brothers, who helped Larry fit in at primary school, would be friends for life.

THE KWONG FAMILY SPOKE THE **CANTONESE** DIALECT OF JUNG SENG.

SECOND MOTHER

Larry's mother worked around the clock to keep the Kwong household running, leaving the house just once a year. Her only outing would be for Chinese New Year to buy special treats like year cake, made of sweet sticky rice. Loo Ying Tow spoke only Cantonese. She did almost all the cooking for the busy family. Larry loved coming home to the smell of her baking bread. She was strict about table manners. A table full of hungry kids was not a problem, because, Larry said, "My mother had her chopsticks ready to knock on us if we got out of hand."

CHINESE UPBRINGING

From a young age Larry was taught how to behave outside the house. "My mom used to say, 'When you go out, you've got to be very, very polite,'" he remembered. For Chinese Canadians at that time, avoiding trouble was especially important since they did not have equal rights or social standing. Larry had to carry a card that identified him as a legal *alien*. He also understood that he was to speak only when spoken to. No drawing attention to himself. "That was the whole Chinese upbringing that, when you're out in public, just be seen and not heard," said Larry. "That's the old Chinese way."

LARRY WAS BORN IN THE YEAR OF THE PIG, ACCORDING TO THE CHINESE ZODIAC. IT IS SAID THAT PIGS WILL STOP AT NOTHING TO ACHIEVE THEIR GOALS.

Two

"HOCKEY NIGHT
IN CHINATOWN"

THE CALL OF HOCKEY

On Saturday nights, the Kwong family gathered around the radio like so many other Canadian families in the 1930s. The big draw was Foster Hewitt. His play-by-play call of National Hockey League action electrified listeners across the country. Over the airwaves, Hewitt transported Larry thousands of miles from Vernon's Chinatown to a great ice palace—Maple Leaf Gardens in Toronto. Hewitt called hockey "the fastest game in the world" and "the king of sports." He pioneered the phrase "He shoots, he scores." Larry jostled for position next to the big wooden radio stand in his living room. He was hooked.

IN 2000 THE ASIAN CANADIAN BAND NUMBER ONE SON RELEASED A SONG ABOUT LARRY KWONG CALLED "HOCKEY NIGHT IN CHINATOWN."

VANCE STREET GARDENS

As soon as the temperature dropped enough, Larry's big brothers Jack and Jimmy would flood the vacant lot on Vance Street with a hose. Once it was frozen, Larry and his siblings would pretend that the humble patch of ice was a big-league arena. Larry's sister Betty would also play with the boys. They would each be a Toronto Maple Leaf, picking one of the names immortalized by Foster Hewitt. Jimmy supplied the hockey sticks. He would collect broken ones from the town rink and fix them up. Boots stood in for goalposts. Horse droppings were frozen into pucks. Larry's hand-me-down skates were several sizes too big, and his stick was held together by tape, but he couldn't stop smiling. "Right away, when I put skates on, I said, 'Gee, I want to be a hockey player,'" Larry said. There were no Chinese Canadians

in *professional* sports, but that didn't stop seven-year-old Larry from shooting for the stars.

TWO SCHOOLS

Larry was not an honor-roll student like his sister Betty or brother Edmund. "I didn't have a favorite [subject] except for sports," confessed Larry. After school was over, Larry would go home for a snack and then report to the Good Angel Mission for two hours of Chinese-language lessons. He had a hard time sitting still there too and was often let out for breaks. "I went out and played marbles instead," said Larry.

CHORES

Larry rushed through his household chores so that he would have more time for hockey and other sports. He would hurriedly chop wood in the backyard, put the small

pieces in a sack and run it to the furnace box. Before bed in the winter, Larry would help carry store items like pickle jars upstairs to prevent them from freezing overnight. Another

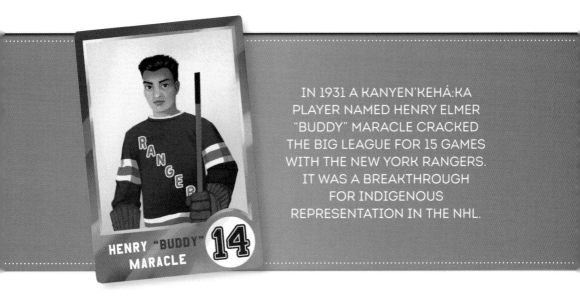

IN 1931 A KANYEN'KEHÁ:KA PLAYER NAMED HENRY ELMER "BUDDY" MARACLE CRACKED THE BIG LEAGUE FOR 15 GAMES WITH THE NEW YORK RANGERS. IT WAS A BREAKTHROUGH FOR INDIGENOUS REPRESENTATION IN THE NHL.

HENRY "BUDDY" MARACLE 14

of Larry's tasks was running to the butcher shop, where he would buy 25 cents' worth of meat for his family's dinner. These physical chores were good training for the budding athlete.

CHINESE HAIR

Larry hoped that the world of hockey would be more accepting of him than some of the places in his hometown. "You had to watch where you [went]," said Larry, "because some stores would not take Chinese as a customer." Vernon's White Lunch restaurant was for white people only. Even getting a haircut could be a challenge. At one barber shop, Larry was told, "We don't cut Chinese hair." That message stayed with Larry. "It was hard to take," he admitted. "I just had to swallow my pride."

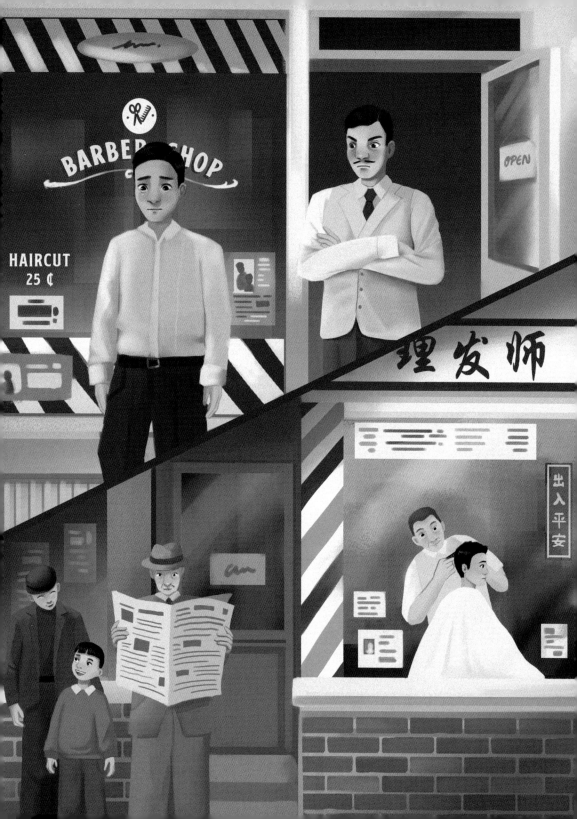

OKANAGAN PRODUCTS

Larry's dream was to be a big-time hockey player. He didn't think about the overwhelming odds against him. No one from Larry's hometown had ever made it to the NHL. The Okanagan Valley was known for producing apples, not hockey players. There were no organized teams for kids in Vernon until high school. The nearest NHL arena was thousands of miles away. For a kid from Vernon, there were no tracks to follow. Larry would have to find his own way to the top of the hockey mountain. While growing up west of the Rockies was a huge obstacle to NHL stardom, there was an even bigger one for Larry—the *color barrier*.

THE COLOR BARRIER

Hockey was commonly known as "a white man's game." When Clarence "Taffy" Abel played with the New York Rangers in 1926, few knew that he was Indigenous. Born to an Ojibwe mother and a white father, Abel hid his ancestry throughout his career for fear of *discrimination*. A racist incident in 1938 showed that there was still an unwritten rule that non-white players weren't welcome in the NHL. That was when Conn Smythe, the owner and manager of the Toronto Maple Leafs, told a brilliant Black player named Herb Carnegie that he would take him for the Leafs, but only if someone could turn him white.

Three

THE CHINA CLIPPER

MUD POND

Larry could never get enough ice time. Vernon didn't have an indoor arena with artificial ice, so Larry prayed for cold weather. Each fall, at the first sign of frost, he and his friends grabbed their hockey gear and hiked high above the orchards for the first ice of the season. At the top of the mountain they would find Mud Pond transformed into a glistening frozen sheet. Larry and the boys would play hockey until sundown and then run back down the mountainside in the dark. One time Larry found the ice rubbery, but he still took his chances on it. Luckily he and his hockey-crazy friends got a skate in without falling through the ice into the frigid water below. When winter set in, they gravitated to other frozen ponds around Vernon.

TOOLS OF THE GAME

In 1934, in the middle of the Great Depression, even a 50-cent hockey stick was a luxury. The Dobie brothers showed Larry how to make his sticks last longer. They would flatten a tin can, fold it over the wooden blade and wrap it up with black electrical tape. To chase his dream, Larry needed decent blades on his feet. "I wore my brother's old skates," said Larry. "I really cried for new ones." In the Eaton's mail-order catalog, new skates cost four dollars. After much begging by Larry, his mom finally agreed to buy him a pair. She ordered a size that would take him years to grow into, but

Men's Skates

4.00 PAIR SPECIAL

Buy them now!

The best value for the winter season!

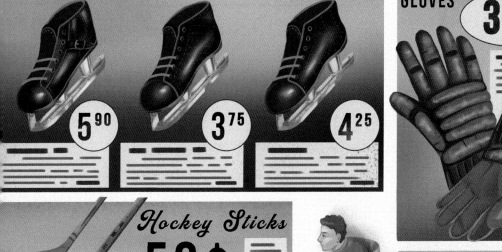

5.90

3.75

4.25

LEATHER HOCKEY GLOVES

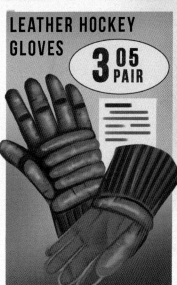

3.05 PAIR

Hockey Sticks

50¢

75¢ PAIR

HOCKEY SWEATERS

2.10 EACH

Larry was grateful. "The family probably suffered because of my skates," he said. "I don't know how my mother got the money."

MAN OF THE MATCH

Next to the Vernon train station was the town's old open-air rink. Larry would go there to cheer on his brother Jimmy, who played defense for Vernon's *junior* hockey team. Larry also watched the men's league games with a keen eye, studying every play. It was a thrill for Larry to skate on the same ice during the drop-in shinny times. Facing off against kids who were older and bigger, Larry began to make a name for himself as a hockey phenom. At age 12 he was invited to join a 14-and-under Vernon team that was just being assembled. Larry's first organized game was in Lumby, against its *rep* team, on January 19, 1936. Even though he was the smallest kid there, a local newspaper called Larry "the outstanding man on the ice." He scored all three of Vernon's goals to give his team a 3–3 tie.

BROKEN HEART

Before Larry could play his next game, he had a sudden fainting spell at home. The doctor found an irregular heartbeat. He told Larry he would have to give up hockey. It was devastating news, but Larry refused to give up on his dream. He kept skating and practicing on his own. In the spring he took up tennis to stay fit.

When winter came around again, Larry's friends joined a new hockey team. Larry followed his doctor's advice and missed the whole 1936–37 season, but he did not lose hope. During the next checkup, the doctor again put his stethoscope to Larry's chest. This time the news brought tears of joy. His heart was sound. He was cleared to play hockey again. Larry Kwong was back in the game.

CIVIC ARENA

On January 6, 1938, a new state-of-the-art arena opened in Vernon. Larry couldn't stop smiling. He marveled at the giant timbers rising to the rafters. Huge lamps blazed high above, and the ice glowed. It all hit home for Larry. No more worrying about the weather.

No more worrying about falling through thin ice on a pond or lake. He had found his place. Looking over the ice, Larry saw a blank sheet that promised endless possibilities.

Soon Larry and his friends became known as rink rats, because they basically lived at the arena. On weekday nights they scraped the ice with big flathead shovels for public skating. In return the boys got free practice ice at six in the morning. One night a few of them hid out after the public skate. Once the rink attendant had locked up, Larry and his pals hit the ice again. They slept in the dressing room and resumed practice first thing in the morning. "It was cold as heck," Larry remembered.

HYDROPHONES

For the 1938–39 season, coach Fred Smith got the local phone and electric company to sponsor Vernon's **midget** team. Larry and the boys were given new sweaters and socks and a new name—the Vernon Hydrophones. Now 15, Larry would finally get to play a full season of rep hockey, including playoffs. The coach's son Les centered the top line with George Dobie and Larry on the wings.

Being the only Chinese player on his team was not

an issue for Larry. His cheerful personality made him popular with his teammates, and they appreciated him as their best player by a long shot. "Team spirit was [coach Fred Smith's] big kick," George said. "He didn't worry about plays particularly. Just turn a guy like Larry loose and let him go." The Hydrophones rang up win after win.

DISHWASHER

Larry's mother didn't think he should be spending his time playing sports when he could be working. To help the family financially, Larry got a part-time job washing dishes at Ming's

Royal Cafe. It was a Chinese restaurant owned by a family friend named Wong Ming. The kitchen was within shouting distance of home, so Larry purposely banged the pots and pans to let his mom know he was keeping busy.

THE PROMISE

Larry eventually convinced his mother to watch him play hockey. "She didn't think too much of it...She thought it was too rough," he remembered. "She said, 'Why do you want to play hockey?' I said, 'Because I can earn some money.'" It was then that a tearful Larry made a desperate but determined promise to his mother. "I will build you a house with my hockey money," he told her.

HIS OWN PATH

For Larry there was no career path except for hockey. By law, Chinese Canadians were not able to be doctors, engineers, lawyers, pharmacists or other professionals. They couldn't get government jobs or vote. The usual occupations of Chinese people in Canada did not appeal to Larry. He respected all the hardworking cooks, cleaners and farm laborers he knew, but Larry wanted something different for himself. "I knew that I couldn't get a job doing other work, because nobody would hire a Chinese," he said. "I thought maybe I could try to make an NHL team."

FLYING HIGH

It wasn't long before Larry picked up the nickname "the China Clipper," after the famous globe-trotting airplane of the 1930s. The kid who could fly all over the ice became a star attraction in rinks around British Columbia. On the road Larry saw signs with ads urging fans to *Come see the China Clipper*. For those hoping to see something special, Larry delivered. His prolific scoring propelled the Hydrophones to the 1939 provincial midget finals against Nelson.

In game one at the Civic Arena, a big crowd cheered in amazement as Larry quickly broke open the game with four solo goals, including two **shorthanded**, in the first period. The Hydrophones didn't look back, sweeping to victory with another Kwong *hat trick* in game two. The young champions were the toast of the town. People were saying that Vernon's China Clipper could go very, very far.

THE *CHINA CLIPPER* WAS A TECHNOLOGICAL MARVEL OF ITS TIME. IN 1935 THE AIRPLANE WAS THE FIRST TO OFFER MAIL DELIVERY ACROSS THE PACIFIC.

THE BORDER

On February 27, 1940, the Hydrophones pulled up to the Canada-US border. Riding a 27-game undefeated streak, they were now on their way to Nelson for the BC *juvenile* championship series. A snowstorm had made roads on the Canadian side impassable, so they needed to go through the United States. The American border guard peered into Fred Smith's car and saw Larry. "He said, 'What's your name? You're Chinese?' I said, 'Yes,' and that's when he said, 'Come out with me.' I went out and he said, 'You can't go.'"

Like Canada, the United States had its own *Chinese Exclusion Act*. No Chinese were allowed to enter. "I had to take a train on the Canadian side by myself," Larry said. He would meet his team down the line. It was a lonely ride. Larry felt helpless and angry. These were supposed to be free countries. But not for

Chinese people like him. Most of the NHL teams were in the United States. How was he going to get past this giant roadblock?

BITTER TASTE

In game one of the 1940 BC juvenile finals, the China Clipper carried on his mission. With Vernon down 3–0 in the first period, Larry sniped three goals in 62 seconds to tie it up. He evened the score once more in the third and then fired the winning goal with less than four minutes to play. After the big game, Larry was still troubled by the border incident. The *Nelson News* reported that the "Chinese bomber" had "all the speed in the world." Larry still worried that **racism** might clip his wings. Nelson came back to win the second game and the championship on total goals scored.

The Nelson press called Larry "the Yellow Threat." That nickname was associated with *yellow peril*, a racist term used to raise fear that Asian people would destroy Western culture.

"That was tough," admitted Larry. "We were winning all the time, and then we lost in that game."

"CHINESE FLASH"

Larry wasn't just a speed demon on the ice. On May 18, 1940, at the Okanagan Valley Schools Track Meet in Vernon, the 16-year-old "Chinese flash" entered the 100-yard dash for competitors age 20 and under. He won easily. Soon after this, Larry was back on the cinder track at Polson Park to run the 100 again with his own age group. Larry crossed the finish line in 10.6 seconds, shattering the Okanagan record by four-tenths of a second.

TENNIS WHITES

That summer Larry qualified for the city tennis championship, which was being held at the Vernon Tennis Club. There was a problem. The club had a strict "no Chinese" rule. A meeting was called, and the members voted to allow Larry to play. For the first time ever, a Chinese person would set foot on the private courts. With that barrier down, Larry breezed through the competition to win the junior title. The next year, in Kamloops, Larry was crowned junior champion of the BC Interior in singles, doubles and mixed doubles.

JUVENILE CROWN

In his final season of minor hockey, Larry wanted to return the Hydrophones to glory. He led them back to the BC juvenile finals in March 1941. This time it was no contest. Larry and his two linemates combined for all of Vernon's goals in a 6–2 game one win over the Kimberley Elks. With four more goals in game two, Larry propelled the Hydrophones to an 8–1 victory and their second provincial title. Full of pride, people in Vernon credited Larry and the boys with putting their town on the map as a provincial hockey power.

SUMMER JOB

After graduating from high school three months later, Larry set about finding a summer job. For years he had helped his brother Jimmy transport produce from the farms to the packing houses. He had worked as a ball boy at the tennis club and as a dishwasher and waiter at Ming's Royal Cafe. With his savings, he had bought a bicycle for his little sister Ina. Now the star of the Hydrophones applied to be a clerk at a Vernon packing house. Larry was told that the owners did not hire Chinese workers. This time the color barrier remained firmly in place.

Four

BLAZING
A TRAIL

SMOKIE HOCKEY

In the middle of the summer of 1941, Larry received an incredible offer. The legendary Trail Smoke Eaters wanted the 18-year-old for their team. They had been the hockey champions of the world only two years earlier! It would be a huge jump from juvenile—over the junior and intermediate ranks—to top-level **senior** hockey. What's more, they were promising a high-paying job at the town's **smelter** alongside the other players. Larry knew that would make his mother happy.

Larry joined the Smoke Eaters and began learning their world-beating brand of hockey. The Trail system involved "a lot of passing, the checkerboard passing," Larry recalled. He eagerly absorbed every pointer the coach and veteran players gave him. A reporter in town wrote, "The only thing that the young athlete fails to excel at is talking about his own accomplishments."

CROWN POINT

All the Smoke Eaters worked up at the smelter operated by Consolidated Mining and Smelting Co., but the team couldn't secure a job there for Larry. The problem, he was told, was his young age. Instead they found Larry a position at the Crown Point Hotel as a bellhop. The smelter job never did pan out. Later Larry found out that the Consolidated company had a rule against hiring Chinese people.

"I felt a little ashamed of myself," said Larry. "But then I said to myself, 'Why am I ashamed? I'm Chinese. That's the way I was born. I was born that from my parents, and I'm proud of them.'" Still, working down at the hotel made Larry feel like he was "not one of the boys." But the hotel's Chinese cook would often wave Larry into the kitchen for a hot meal of noodles and vegetables. Larry appreciated that. And then it was back to work, lugging suitcases in the shadow of the big, belching smokestacks.

35

SENIOR PLAYERS WERE CLASSIFIED AS *AMATEUR*, MEANING THEY WERE NOT SUPPOSED TO BE PAID TO PLAY. BUT TEAMS MADE SURE THAT THEIR ATHLETES GOT PAYCHECKS. A ROSTER SPOT WOULD COME WITH A JOB AT A LOCAL COMPANY. IN LARRY'S DAY, THESE "AMATEURS" COULD MAKE EVEN MORE MONEY THAN PLAYERS IN THE NHL.

ROOKIE SENSATION

On the ice Larry fit right in, surprising people with his speed, tricky moves with the puck and smoking shot. As a rookie, he started on Trail's third line. Promoted to the top line in January 1942, Larry caught fire and lit up the opposition for 7 goals and 10 points during a six-game streak. He was a crowd favorite and the talk of the league.

But Larry's promising start in Trail was cut short by World War II. In March 1942, the Smoke Eaters shut down for the rest of the war, leaving a disappointed Larry to find a new team and a new job.

NANAIMO CLIPPER

The China Clipper landed next in Nanaimo, where he would star for a senior team fittingly called the Clippers. The Vancouver Island Senior Hockey League boasted NHL talents such as Hall of Famer Charlie Rayner, who were playing out the war on

Vernon News

SECOND WORLD WAR BEGINS
•CANADA AT WAR WITH GERMANY•

FRANCE INVADED

DRAFTING TO BEGIN SOON

GUNFIRE ON WESTERN FRONT

military teams. Larry was excited to match his skills against some of the best. Larry's day job in the winter of 1942–43 was at Newcastle Shipbuilding, making minesweepers. "It's cold," he said. "You're up by the ocean, damp. We had to nail corks in the wall of the ship. You nail the cork in and then you shave it off. And it's windy. Then you had to play hockey that night."

TEEN IDOL

Suddenly hundreds of Chinese Canadians were showing up at Larry's games. Still a teen, Larry had to get used to the idea that these fans saw him as a role model. He was flattered and tried to make them proud. Larry made his mark as one of the hottest

players in the league down the stretch. In the last five games of the season, Larry scored a goal in each and added six assists. But after the season the Clippers also folded because of the war. Once again Larry had to move on.

ANXIOUS TIMES

Larry returned to Vernon, where things were tense in the Kwong household. War was raging in China, and Larry's brother Harry was stuck there with his wife, Sue, and son, Kenny, because of the Exclusion Act. First Mother was sick with worry. Larry's sister Eva was leading the fundraising campaign in Vernon for Chinese war relief. Finally they got word that Harry and his family were safe. First Mother passed away not long after, on July 8, 1943, at age 59.

PROFESSIONAL HOCKEY

In the meantime word had traveled across the continent about the hockey prowess of Larry Kwong. In Cleveland, Hockey Hall of Famer Bill Cook was trying to assemble another championship team in the American Hockey League (AHL), the main farm league of the NHL. Cook sent an offer to Larry. Would he like to turn pro with the Cleveland Barons? Would he like to be paid just to play the game? Larry's answer was a resounding yes. In the AHL he'd be watched closely by big-league scouts. The National Hockey League would be just one step away.

DENIED

Larry was all set to go, but to his dismay the Canadian government refused to let him leave the country to play in the AHL. Larry was told he had to stay in Canada in case he was drafted to fight in the war, even though Chinese Canadians had been excluded from the *draft* since World War I. In 1943 they still weren't wanted. This time Larry was not going to quietly accept being held back. He reached out to Cyclone Taylor for help. Cyclone, who was the top *immigration* official in Vancouver, had been one of hockey's first superstars. He had been a vocal supporter of Larry since seeing him skate circles around the opposition with the Hydrophones. Cyclone argued on Larry's behalf, but the ruling stood. Larry's brother Jack wrote a letter of appeal to the government. Much to Larry's frustration, he was denied again.

VANCOUVER

Larry didn't have to look far to find another team. The owner of Vancouver's senior hockey club jumped at the chance to sign him. In the Pacific Coast Senior Hockey League, Larry would again go head-to-head against NHL players on military squads. By day Larry worked in a coffee shop, and by night he was described as "one of the most feared attackers" in the league. His dominating performances on the ice made him a folk hero to Vancouver's large Chinese Canadian community. With glowing reports in the press,

Larry was in the spotlight. He told reporter Alf Cottrell how the attention could be a good and bad thing: "The fans like to see a Chinese hockey player as a curiosity. That's my good luck. But it has its disadvantages. Ever since I was a midget there has always been a player or two trying to cut off my head just because I am Chinese. And the bigger the league, the bigger the axe they use!"

Larry kept his head and led his team in goals. The Vancouver press used many superlatives to describe how he performed on the ice, including

"Larry Kwong is a big league comer if there ever was one," said a reporter for the *Vancouver News-Herald*. They said he was destined for the NHL. But his hockey career came to a halt again in January 1944, when the Pacific Coast League stopped operations because of the war.

DRAFTED

Back home in Vernon, Larry was shocked to receive his draft letter for the Canadian Army. The government had finally decided to conscript Chinese Canadians to use them for top-secret commando missions in Southeast Asia. They were to be dropped into jungles, behind enemy lines, to disrupt the Japanese forces. It was assumed that they would "blend in," even if they couldn't speak the local languages. Now Larry would have to put his hockey dreams on hold and put his life on the line. "I wasn't prepared, no," he admitted. "I knew we couldn't vote, but it didn't enter my mind that I wouldn't go. You have to do what the country asks you."

BOOT CAMP

Larry reported for basic training in Red Deer, Alberta. Boot camp was an eye-opening experience for him. "You had to get up at nighttime to go out [for training]," he remembered. "Then they were firing live shots at us and we had to keep our heads down. I kept mine down, I can tell you that."

After all the drills, Private Kwong was informed that he was not going to be deployed overseas after all. "They came up and said, 'You're not going to go on with the army,'" Larry recalled. "'You're going to stay here and play hockey for the team to entertain the troops.'" He was thrilled by his new marching orders.

WAR GAMES

Larry teamed up with NHL pros on the Red Deer Army Wheelers to go up against Hall of Famer Max Bentley and a stacked Calgary Currie Army team in the 1944 Alberta National Defense Hockey League finals. Despite his team losing both games, Larry showed that he belonged with the big leaguers. Scoring a goal and two assists, Larry was singled out by one reporter as "the only Wheeler who matched Currie's speed."

Larry was then sent to another Alberta base and saw action with the Wetaskiwin Army Colonels in the 1944–45 hockey season. He put on some amazing scoring exhibitions. In one game, Larry outmaneuvered a Royal Canadian Air Force team to score seven goals, including six in the third period alone, in a 9–3 win. Two days before his 22nd birthday, Larry Kwong was proud to be promoted to the rank of corporal in the Canadian Army.

RETURN TO TRAIL

When the war ended in 1945, Larry was released from duty. He rejoined the Smoke Eaters in Trail for another run at the Allan Cup. The smelter still would not give Larry a job, but the team yearbook said he "won the hearts of Trail hockey fans with his clever play and brilliance around the net." Larry finished in the top six in league scoring. But his point total should have been even higher, claimed team president Ed Benson, who noticed that a scorekeeper in one of the opposition rinks had the suspicious habit of not recording Larry's assists.

SCOUTED

In the 1946 playoffs, Larry led Trail with 11 goals. In the fifth and deciding game of the BC senior finals, Larry came through with the winning goal against New Westminster. His late-game heroics gave Trail the Savage Cup and sent them through to the Allan Cup semifinals. They lost the series to Calgary, but not before Larry caught the eye of scout Henry Viney. He convinced Frank Boucher, the manager and coach of the New York Rangers, to offer Larry an NHL tryout.

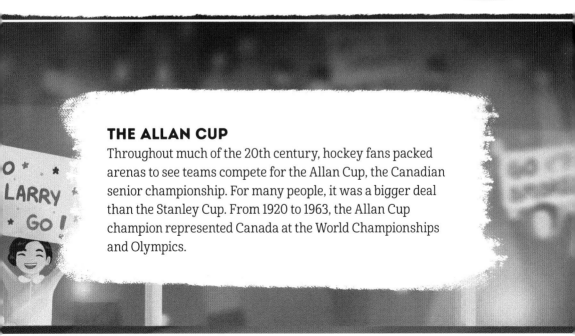

THE ALLAN CUP

Throughout much of the 20th century, hockey fans packed arenas to see teams compete for the Allan Cup, the Canadian senior championship. For many people, it was a bigger deal than the Stanley Cup. From 1920 to 1963, the Allan Cup champion represented Canada at the World Championships and Olympics.

Five

KING
KWONG

ICE SKAT
MADISON SQ. GARDEN
MADISON SQ.
GARDEN
MARCH 16TH
JAMAICA HAWKS
VS
BROOKLYN TORPEDOES
NEW YORK ROVERS
VS
WASHINGTON LIONS

NHL TRYOUT

Larry's hands trembled as he held the letter from the Rangers. His big break had come at last.

"This is the chance Kwong has been waiting for ever since the day he chased a puck on Vernon's ice fields," wrote Larry's best friend, George Dobie, who covered the story as a reporter for the British United Press.

At the Rangers tryouts in Winnipeg, Larry battled close to 70 other prospects from across Canada over four days. Passing every test with flying colors, Larry won a contract to start on their *farm team*, the New York Rovers. If Larry proved himself there, he'd get his NHL shot.

"Coach Boucher thinks I have a good chance to make the NHL after I get some experience with the Rovers," Larry told CBC Radio's Walt Randall.

Do you think you can make the grade in professional hockey, Larry?" Randall asked.

"Yes, I think I can, Walt."

SEASON OPENER

After the Rovers' training camp in Windsor, Ontario, the team traveled into the United States to start their season. This time Larry was allowed to cross the border. The United States had repealed its Chinese Exclusion Act in 1943, though Canada's remained. Larry's first game for the Rovers was in Boston on October 27, 1946. A large group of Chinese Americans came to cheer Larry on against the Olympics, the Eastern Amateur Hockey League's defending champions. In the second period, they went wild when Larry intercepted a pass and blasted a shot from 30 feet (9 meters) out into the Boston net. After the game Larry was delighted to be the guest of honor at a big party in Boston's Chinatown.

THE BIG APPLE

For Larry, it was quite a change to go from the apple orchards of Vernon to the skyscrapers of the Big Apple. Larry joked that he got a stiff neck from looking up at all the tall buildings. It was also something new for New Yorkers to see a Chinese hockey player. As word spread of Larry's big talent, fans flocked to Madison Square Garden. The Rovers were used to drawing 2,500 attendees to their afternoon games. With King Kwong on board, it wasn't long before they were bringing in more than 15,000—a crowd three times the population of his hometown. When Larry got the puck, he brought people to their feet.

King Kwong is a pun on *King Kong*, a 1933 blockbuster movie about a giant ape brought to New York to be a Broadway attraction. Kong breaks free and goes on a rampage, famously climbing the Empire State Building before being shot down.

KEY TO CHINATOWN

Larry was an idol to the legions of Chinese fans who came to see him play. For many, it was their first time watching hockey. To see one of their own making good on a big stage was an enormous thrill. Larry was climbing the ladder of success, and that gave people hope. The Chinese community had been kept down for so long.

King Kwong was breaking new ground in the field of sports. At the time, many Westerners thought Asians were physically inferior and couldn't be athletes. Larry busted those stereotypes with his hockey stick. November 17, 1946, was Larry Kwong Day at Madison Square Garden. In front of a big crowd, Larry humbly skated to center ice before the game to receive a very special honor. Shavey Lee, the unofficial mayor of New York's Chinese community, made Larry an honorary citizen and presented him with the Key to Chinatown.

CHINESE FANS OFTEN CHEERED LARRY ON BY CALLING OUT "DING HAO!" WHICH MEANS "THE BEST."

GOING UP?

Larry showed a knack for scoring at key times—first goals to break the ice as well as dramatic game winners. Eastern Amateur Hockey League goalies rated Larry's shot as the toughest to stop. In January 1947, Larry's hopes were boosted as rumors swirled in the media that he would soon be called up to the Rangers. Larry was poised to break the NHL's color barrier and become the first player of Asian descent in the league. But the Rangers opted to bring up two other Rover forwards instead of him. Larry eagerly awaited his turn. In the playoffs he led the Rovers with seven goals in nine games. Nine days after Larry's season ended without an NHL call-up, Jackie Robinson made history, becoming the first Black player in Major League Baseball. "I was really cheering for him," said Larry.

JACKIE ROBINSON 42

PROMISE KEPT

Putting his dream on hold for the summer, Larry rejoined his family in Calgary, where they had moved. He hadn't forgotten his childhood promise to his mother. She had made countless sacrifices. She had let him carve out his own path in life. Now he could do something big for her. In the lot beside his brother Jack's place, Larry built his mother a house with the money he had made from playing hockey.

THE RETURN OF KING KWONG

Larry returned to the Rovers in the fall of 1947, confident that his NHL chance was near. That year the Rovers opted to play in both the rough-and-tumble Eastern Amateur Hockey League and the fast and powerful Quebec Senior Hockey League. The vast majority of Larry's games were on the road, played in front of hostile crowds. On Sundays he often had to play twice. "It takes a lot out of one!" Larry said of the double schedule. If he was tired, it didn't show on the ice. He just kept piling up the points.

WAITING

Still Larry waited for the Rangers' call. He watched as player after player was promoted to the NHL ahead of him. Larry didn't know what more he could do. To make the NHL, he had worked hard to excel in all areas of the game. Larry's elite speed, stickhandling and shot were only part of the package. Coach Fred Metcalfe considered him one of the best passers and smartest all-around players he had ever coached. Larry was also a superb checker, adept at breaking up plays and stealing the puck. He could play an aggressive, crashing game and handle any rough stuff. Plus, he was extremely popular with his teammates. Nobody in the Rangers organization had any advice for him to get to the next level. "They didn't try to change me at all," Larry said. In February, Rover winger Fern Perreault was called up for two games with the Rangers, even though Larry had scored more than twice as many points as Perreault in their Quebec Senior Hockey League games.

TEAM MVP

That season Larry racked up more points than any Rover had in almost a decade. New York fans voted him the team's most valuable player (MVP) of the year. On March 7, 1948, he received his prize, a wristwatch, from the Rovers' fan club. That night the Rangers needed another forward to go up against Gordie "Mr. Hockey" Howe and the Detroit Red Wings. Again they passed over Larry, inviting his roommate Hub Anslow to join them instead. At the time Larry didn't complain, but many years later he shared his feelings. "Definitely I should've been up there," he said. "I was the leading scorer, and yet they pull everybody else up before me."

GORDIE HOWE "MR. HOCKEY" 9

COACH STRICKEN

The Rovers opened the playoffs in Valleyfield, Quebec, on March 9, 1948, losing game one in overtime. The next day Fred Metcalfe didn't show up for the team's morning meeting. Alarmed, Larry and his teammates pushed their way into Fred's hotel room to find him collapsed on the floor. He'd suffered a heart attack. Larry's mentor was rushed to the hospital.

THE CALL

Back in New York on March 12, a worried Larry was told that his big chance had finally arrived. He would join the Rangers in Montreal for a game against the Canadiens. "I was telling myself, 'I finally made it,'" he said. "This is what I had dreamed about since I was a little kid."

HOSPITAL VISIT

Before the big game, Larry went to see Fred Metcalfe, who was recovering at Royal Victoria Hospital in Montreal. "He said to me, 'Larry, they finally brought you up. You should've been up there a long time ago.' That's what he told me. And I trust his word because he was one of my best coaches."

PUBLICITY

Larry's call-up made international headlines. "It was in the papers through the whole of Canada that I was going up," he said. The story also ran from coast to coast in the States. "I was very nervous," said Larry. "We had lots of publicity on it—being the first Chinese to play in the NHL."

FROM 1942 TO 1967 THERE WERE ONLY SIX TEAMS IN THE NHL. THAT MEANT THERE WERE LESS THAN 100 ROSTER SPOTS. TO MAKE THE LEAGUE IN THE *ORIGINAL SIX* ERA WAS AN INCREDIBLE ACHIEVEMENT.

THE DRESSING ROOM

Deep in the Montreal Forum, Larry suited up in the visitors' dressing room. He put his left skate on first, as he did before every game. Skates tied, Larry proudly pulled on his Rangers sweater. When it was time, he grabbed one of his sticks. "When I

have a stick in my hand, I know that is the one," he said. "There's something to it that I can feel." With their sticks, the other Blueshirts gave Larry taps of encouragement on his shin pads. Larry remembered NHL scoring leader Buddy O'Connor telling him, "Do your best."

LARRY WORE THE NUMBER 8 IN HIS NHL DEBUT.

THE MONTREAL FORUM

Built in 1924, the Montreal Forum was the oldest of the Original Six arenas and the home of the Montreal Canadiens for 70 seasons. Montreal established a tradition of excellence over that span, hosting the Stanley Cup finals 32 times and winning 24 Cups. Over the years it was said that the ghosts of the Forum would make the bounces go the Canadiens' way.

MAURICE "ROCKET" RICHARD 9

FIRST PERIOD

The game began with Larry on the bench, watching Maurice "Rocket" Richard and the other stars. Larry waited to jump over the boards to join them. "When you go to the Montreal Forum, the crowd are all yelling and really bustling," Larry remembered. "The Forum was built so that noise seemed to carry from one section to another."

The Rangers rolled three forward lines while Larry sat. He was the odd man out. Nearing the midway mark of the first period, winger Tony Leswick was sent to the penalty box for 12 minutes. That left the Rangers with nine forwards. Still Larry did not get on the ice. The first period came and went without a single shift for Larry.

SECOND PERIOD

The Canadiens opened the scoring in the second period. The Rangers offense was not clicking. Still coach Frank Boucher

would not give Larry a shot. "I was wanting to get on the ice to show what I can do," he said. Larry remained glued to the bench for the entire second period.

THIRD PERIOD

Another goal made it 2–0 for the Canadiens, but the Rangers answered back with two quick ones of their own. The game was tied. Still riding the pine, Larry watched helplessly as Montreal scored the go-ahead goal with only 3:35 remaining.

"Waiting and waiting and waiting," Larry said. "Just sitting there waiting, at the end of the bench." Larry's big game had turned into a bad dream.

THE SHIFT

With time slipping away, Coach Boucher called for a change. "And just at the last minute he threw me in," said Larry. His moment

had come. Larry leapt over the boards and suddenly the NHL had a new face—its first player of Asian descent. Larry had broken the color barrier. Against all odds, the kid from a humble Chinatown had made the giant leap to the highest level possible. Larry gained control of the puck and snapped a pass to an open teammate. For a magical minute, Larry blazed over the ice like a shooting star.

GAME OVER

The final buzzer sounded. The Canadiens held on to win 3–2. After the loss Larry was sent back down to the Rovers without explanation. For the rest of Larry's life, it was hard for him to speak of that night in Montreal. "How can you prove yourself in a minute on the ice?" he asked journalist Tom Hawthorn 53 years later. "Couldn't even get warmed up."

SEEING RED

"King for a Day" joked one New York headline about Larry's brief time with the Blueshirts.

"I was very disappointed I didn't get a better chance to prove myself," Larry said. Taking Larry's place in the Rangers lineup was 34-year-old Rover winger Herb Foster, who had managed only 12 points in 21 Quebec Senior Hockey League games. Back with the Rovers, Larry felt used. "The Rangers got what they wanted," admitted their public relations director John Halligan many years later. "They got noticed!"

Hockey historian Stan Fischler said, "There was no justice for Larry Kwong. He deserved better."

BRAVE MOVE

After the season was over, Larry was a *free agent*. The Rangers wanted to keep him in their farm system. Offers came in from other top senior teams. The owner of the Valleyfield Braves, Arthur Vinet, had told Larry, "Anytime you want a job, you give me a call. We want you here."

Larry needed a change. "As soon as I knew I wouldn't get a chance with the Rangers...I phoned right away to Valleyfield," said Larry. "They gave me a better contract."

Seven

BRAVE HERO

UNDERDOGS

Valleyfield (now called Salaberry-de-Valleyfield) was the smallest city in the Quebec Senior Hockey League (QSHL). For a town of less than 25,000 people to go up against big cities like New York, Montreal and Boston was seemingly a giant mismatch. Wins had been hard to come by for the Valleyfield Braves in the team's three years in the QSHL. Larry was determined to change that. Le Petit Chinois, as he was known in Quebec, was up to the challenge. He was used to being an underdog and beating the odds. Twenty-five years old and in his hockey prime, Larry was also playing for another chance at the big league. Most of the Montreal Canadiens had come up through the QSHL. Larry would try to make it impossible for NHL teams to overlook him.

OVER THE ROVERS

Larry carried some extra motivation into his first game as a Brave. In the 1948–49 season opener, he came back to haunt his old team in New York, scoring a goal and setting up the game winner late in the third period. When the Rovers visited in late December, Larry burned them again, leading Valleyfield to a runaway victory with a hat trick in the first period. "Why did we ever let Kwong go?" complained the Rangers' business manager, Tommy Lockhart, as reported in a Valleyfield Braves game program. "We must be crazy!"

KWONG'S OFFICE

Larry Kwong was renowned for his creativity on the ice. When the Great One, Wayne Gretzky, the NHL's all-time leading scorer, came along years later, he reminded some people of Larry. Sports historian Gaston Legault credited Larry with inventing the concept that was later known as "Gretzky's office"—using the space behind the opposition's net to make assists. Larry's teammate Bert Bourassa also saw the similarity. "He made extraordinary passes from the back of the net," said Bourassa. In the 1980s, when Gretzky was setting up in his "office," it was seen as a new strategy, but Larry had done it 30 years earlier.

LEADING THE WAY

Larry's playmaking helped the Valleyfield Braves nearly double their wins from the year before. Larry waited for an NHL team to call, but there was only silence. Another strong season with the Braves in 1949–50 drew no NHL offers for him. Larry returned to Valleyfield for 1950–51, determined to take his game to an even higher level and bring the city its first championship. Early in the season, Larry's teammates voted to make him an alternate captain.

The *A* on Larry's sweater was a milestone, coming at a time before a single Asian Canadian had been elected to public office. To see a Chinese Canadian in a leadership role on one of the best hockey teams in the country was groundbreaking. "I was very proud and tried to be a good leader," said Larry. Valleyfield's coach, Toe Blake, considered Larry untouchable. "I would not trade Kwong under any circumstances," said the Hall of Famer.

CASUAL RACISM

Larry had earned the respect of his peers. He had gained many fans. But casual racism was still a part of his day-to-day life. "We would go into a restaurant or something, and because he was Chinese they would joke and kid with him...in a bad way," said his teammate Bingo Ernst. "So I would tell them, 'You respect this man. He's my friend.'"

HOSTILE RECEPTION

Larry was used to hearing racial slurs in opposition rinks. "You take it for granted that the opponent players or fans would call you that," he said. On December 2, 1950, a fan in Chicoutimi, Quebec, would not stop spewing racist insults at Larry. Finally the man grabbed Larry to keep him from getting onto the ice. A scuffle ensued. Three Chicoutimi players attacked Larry. Bingo Ernst jumped in and helped fight them off. Larry shook off the incident, scoring the winning goal one night later against the Quebec Aces in Quebec City.

SIZE ISSUE

Larry "is not a big man," said coach Frank Boucher. "But he's no runt, and smaller men have made good in the NHL." Larry was 5'6" and 150 pounds, while the average NHL player in 1948 was 5'10" and 174 pounds. That year the NHL's MVP, Buddy O'Connor, was about Larry's size. Being a smaller player in hockey has always been a challenge, but Larry constantly showed he had the speed and skill to outdo bigger men. He just wasn't given the chance to do that in the NHL.

TITLES ON THE LINE

Larry was in a tight race for the league scoring title that season. On January 14, 1951, he was credited with an assist in a game against Shawinigan, Quebec, that would have put him into the lead. Knowing that it was a mistake, Larry unselfishly told the scorekeeper, and the point was given to the right teammate. That night he produced four more points to take first place honestly.

Most important to Larry, however, was his team's quest to finish atop the standings. "The main thing is to win the title for the team," Larry wrote to his brother Jack. Larry ended up tying for the most assists in the league, and he finished a close second in the scoring race with 85 points in 60 games.

BANNER YEAR

Larry and the Braves cruised to their first regular-season pennant. In the semifinals, all-time great goalie Jacques Plante could not stop Valleyfield from eliminating his Montreal Royals. Standing in the Braves' way now were the Quebec Aces, led by the legendary Herb Carnegie and Hall of Fame coach Punch Imlach. In game one of the best-of-nine finals, Le Petit Chinois was the hero, firing the winning goal from a sharp angle in double overtime. The deciding game nine also went into overtime. Larry's teammate Georges Bougie ended it, sending the Valleyfield crowd into pandemonium. Little Valleyfield had taken the crown.

THE NATIONAL STAGE

The Braves would now play for the Canadian title. Larry had won provincial titles before, but never a national one. A new trophy called the Alexander Cup was replacing the Allan Cup as the top prize in Canadian major senior hockey. The 1951 championship pitted Valleyfield against the Toronto St. Michael's Monarchs. The games were at the Montreal Forum and at the arena of Larry's childhood dreams, Maple Leaf Gardens. As the series went back and forth, Larry thrilled fans in both hockey shrines with timely goals and assists. With a game-six win on Toronto ice,

Larry and the Braves clinched the title and the first Alexander Cup. The celebrations in Valleyfield lasted for 10 days. For the first time a Chinese Canadian was a national hockey champion.

LEAGUE MVP

That magical season Larry was named the Quebec Senior Hockey League's First All-Star Team center. He was also picked as the league's most valuable player (MVP), an award that was seen as a ticket to the NHL.

"The China Clipper is perhaps the best all-round player in the QSHL, possibly in Canadian senior hockey," wrote Frank Selke Jr., the Montreal Forum's publicity director, in May 1951. Selke's father was

the general manager of the Montreal Canadiens. Larry hoped to hear from him. He was dominating senior hockey and had helped Valleyfield pull off a true Cinderella story. But still there was no invitation to the big time for him.

> IN 2001, 50 YEARS AFTER THE BRAVES' HISTORIC WIN, THE CITY OF VALLEYFIELD INVITED LARRY AND HIS TEAMMATES BACK FOR A CELEBRATION TO COMMEMORATE THEIR CANADIAN CHAMPIONSHIP VICTORY.

BIG NAME RECOGNITION

The 1951–52 season was another stellar one for Larry as he challenged rising superstar Jean Béliveau for the league goal-

JEAN BÉLIVEAU 4

scoring title, his 38 goals second only to Jean's 45. Jean Béliveau would go on to become one of the NHL's all-time greats, winning two goal-scoring titles, two MVP awards plus one for the playoffs, and 10 Stanley Cups with the Canadiens. When asked many years later about Larry Kwong, Jean rated him among the best: "What makes a great hockey player is when you have a talent for the game," he said. "You use it well, work hard.

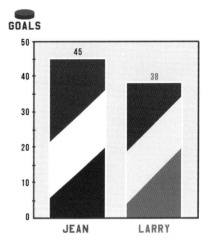

GOALS

That's what makes you in a class [above]. That's where he was."

In his first five years in the Quebec Senior Hockey League, Larry had scored the second-most points. In that time the NHL had pulled up more than 20 forwards from the league. One of those players was Hall of Famer Dickie Moore, who expressed wonder at why Larry wasn't called up. "Larry was a heck of a hockey player," he told journalist David Davis. "He was a good skater, a good puck handler. He could score goals. What more do they want?"

No matter how well Larry played, it was racism that made it impossible for him to have a career in the NHL. The league wasn't ready to accept someone who looked like Larry. In 1948 he had been the only non-white player in the NHL for all of a minute. It would be 10 more years before the first Black player, Willie O'Ree, played in the league.

LARRY KWONG'S RESTAURANT

Larry was very busy off the ice too. In March 1952 he opened his own restaurant in Valleyfield, serving Chinese and Western food. Riding on the back of his celebrity, the restaurant was a bustling success with a staff of 32.

MOVING ON

Hockey was a difficult business to maintain in Valleyfield, as the arena could seat only 2,000 spectators. In 1955 the team folded. Before moving on with his hockey career, Larry gave a speech at the Chamber of Commerce to thank the people of Valleyfield for their support.

"Valleyfield did not impress me at first," he said, "but I have found out since that it is not the tall buildings or neon lights that make a city, but it is the people themselves. I came from the West, where we are proud of and boast about that trademark Western hospitality, but I can sincerely say that the French Canadian people and particularly the people of Valleyfield do not have to take a back seat in that respect."

Larry suited up for three more teams before receiving an offer to take his talents to England in 1957. "I was all for it because I wanted to travel," he said. Larry had turned down Britain's top hockey league eight years earlier because he kept waiting for his chance to play again in the NHL. Now 34, he knew that his chance had passed.

Eight

HOCKEY AMBASSADOR

NOTTINGHAM PANTHER

In 1957 Larry left the restaurant behind and took his game overseas. He was far from finished with hockey. Larry made an immediate impact in the British National League.

Scoring on his first shift as a Nottingham Panther, he went on to notch 55 goals in 55 games. "'Superstar' is not enough to describe Kwong!" raved British goal judge Baz Shaw.

"I like it here," Larry told *Ice Hockey World and Skating Review* magazine. "The people are kind and understanding. The hockey is smart, and I play with a great bunch of fellas. What more can a man ask?"

AUDREY

Larry was waiting for a practice at the Nottingham arena when someone on the ice caught his eye. Her name was Audrey Craven. "She was doing fancy skating and she was practicing," Larry said. The pair met and fell in love. But because Audrey was white, many people didn't approve of their relationship. "They don't say it right to your face," Larry said, "but you hear that they talk about you behind your back."

LAND OF THE ALPS

After electrifying British hockey for a season, Larry was persuaded to take on a new challenge—developing hockey in Switzerland, where most games were still played on outdoor rinks. Larry took over the Ambrì-Piotta hockey club in the Switzerland National League A, making him the first person of Asian descent to coach a European senior hockey team. Larry not only coached but led his club in scoring in 1958–59, with 19 goals and 30 points in 14 games. He was a sensation throughout the country. As one Swiss sportswriter put it, he was the most spectacular hockey player one could dream of.

SWISS CANADIANS

"We used to form a team called 'Swiss Canadians,'" Larry recalled proudly. Joining Larry were other **player-coaches** from Canada. He was the only one with NHL experience. In November 1958, the Swiss Canadians easily beat Scottish and Italian teams to capture a tournament in Geneva. They barnstormed the country, putting on magnificent exhibitions of hockey against Swiss clubs. In the deciding game of the 1959 Auto Salon Cup tournament, Larry and the Swiss Canadians went up against the Czechoslovakian national team that had just won bronze at the 1959 Ice Hockey World Championships. Larry scored twice, including the game winner, in a 5–3 victory.

COACH KWONG

In 1959 the Swiss Ice Hockey Federation banned foreign players in order to open more spots for players born in Switzerland. Larry decided to stay in the country anyway to coach Hockey Club Lugano. Still acrobatic at 36, he continued to star in friendly matches organized to promote hockey in the country. Larry teamed up with the Swiss Canadians again in March 1960 to defeat Europe's top two national squads, the Soviet Union and Czechoslovakia. He coached Swiss clubs throughout most of the 1960s. He also worked as a physical-education teacher and a tennis pro in Lausanne. Swiss Ice Hockey Federation CEO Patrick Bloch called Larry "a great ambassador and builder of hockey."

RETURN TO CANADA

Larry and Audrey married in 1964 and welcomed their daughter, Kristina, four years later. In 1972 the three left Switzerland to settle in Calgary. Larry teamed up with his brother Jack to run two popular Food-Vale grocery stores. The business thrived, but tragedy struck in 1979 when Audrey died of cancer at age 50. Larry was devastated but now had to focus on being a father to his 11-year-old daughter.

GOOD CITIZEN

Larry stayed active, sharing his love of sports with his daughter, nieces and friends. "Sport will develop good citizens," Larry said. He also dedicated himself to community service with the Rotary Club in Calgary. "You feel good helping different people," he said. In 1997, 25 years after leaving Switzerland, Larry was invited back to be recognized as a pioneer and key figure in the development of Swiss hockey. In 2002 Larry was honored with Calgary's Asian Heritage Month Award as a "role model for Chinese Canadians and Calgarians."

RESILIENCE

Larry's extraordinary life was touched by more tragedy. Ten years after losing his wife, Audrey, Larry had married an old friend from Valleyfield named Janine Boyer. Sadly, she died in 1999. In his old age, Larry had both legs amputated because of diabetes. Despite these terrible personal losses, Larry always stayed positive. He adored his two granddaughters, Samantha and Madison. He didn't dwell on the disappointment of that night in Montreal in

MIKE WONG

It took 27 years for another player of Asian descent to reach the NHL. Mike Wong, a Minnesotan with Chinese and Native American heritage, played 22 games for the Detroit Red Wings in the 1975-76 season.

1948 either. "Keep smiling," he liked to say. Even in his later years, Larry was always quick to flash his famous smile.

RECOGNITION

Over time Larry Kwong's fame faded. But in 2009, at the age of 85, Larry returned to his hometown of Vernon to be honored at an elementary school and a junior hockey game. Ten-year-old Gavin Donald heard Larry's story and took action—he nominated his new hero to be inducted into the British Columbia Sports Hall of Fame. Bob Nicholson was the Hockey Canada president and CEO at the time. "There are very few figures in Canadian hockey that have made an impact like that of Mr. Kwong," he said.

In his letter of support, Ken King, then president and CEO of the Calgary Flames, added, "The NHL has produced many stories of individuals with determination to break down barriers and with perseverance to overcome obstacles, but Larry Kwong's story is such a tremendous example of those qualities. Mr. Kwong has the qualities of character that force open eyes and doors, resulting in a better sport and a better world."

After so many years, Larry was delighted to be inducted into the BC

Sports Hall of Fame, Okanagan Sports Hall of Fame and Alberta Hockey Hall of Fame. "I thought my sports career was ancient history," he said with a chuckle.

THE SWEATER LARRY WORE FOR THE NANAIMO CLIPPERS IS ON DISPLAY IN THE HOCKEY HALL OF FAME IN TORONTO.

CROWNING ACHIEVEMENT

In 2013 a documentary about Larry's life and career was made. "If I was young again, I would do exactly what I did," Larry told filmmaker Chester Sit. Larry Kwong was more than a long shot to make it big in hockey. But that was Larry's dream, and he gave it his best shot. That shot made history and changed the game. The unstoppable sniper triggered a shift in society too, by showing that stereotypes and color barriers could be broken. Today unfairness persists in many forms. Like Larry, we can keep shooting to make things better.

SPORTS HEROES

Larry Kwong and other Asian sports trailblazers, such as Walter Achiu, Andy Tommy Sr., Sammy Lee, Vicki Draves, George Chin and Normie Kwong, paved the way for more recent stars like Vicky Sunohara, Kristi Yamaguchi, Michael Chang, Paul Kariya, Michelle Kwan, Carol Huynh, Julie Chu, Apolo Ohno, Jeremy Lin, Patrick Chan, Nathan Chen, Suni Lee and Jason Robertson.

Larry passed away peacefully in 2018 at the age of 94. In Canada's House of Commons, MP Michael Chong stood up to pay tribute. "My generation owes a great deal to Larry Kwong. He blazed a trail so that others could follow. I stand here today because I stand on the shoulders of giants like Larry Kwong." Larry Kwong wasn't just a champion of hockey. He was a champion of diversity and fair play for all.

1917–18: The first season of the National Hockey League (NHL) is played.

December 31, 1918: Paul Jacobs becomes the first Indigenous player on an NHL roster. He is credited with one game for the Toronto Arenas.

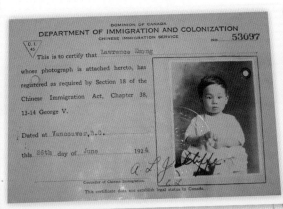

June 17, 1923: Lawrence Kwong (Eng Kai Geong) is born in Vernon, British Columbia.

July 1, 1923: Canada passes the Chinese Immigration Act (also known as the Chinese Exclusion Act), barring Chinese people from entering the country.

November 16, 1926: Clarence "Taffy" Abel makes his NHL debut. He hides his Indigenous heritage during his hockey career to avoid racial discrimination.

1929: Larry's father, Ng Shu Kwong, passes away, and the Great Depression begins.

1938–41: Larry becomes known as the China Clipper and leads the Vernon Hydrophones to two BC provincial hockey championships.

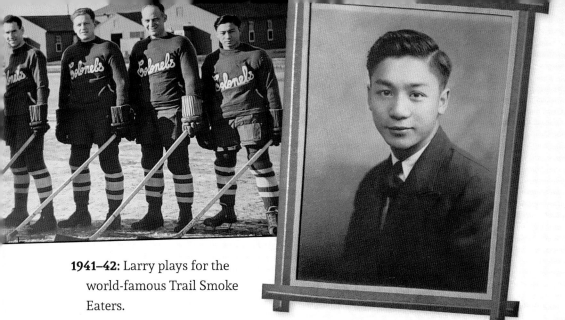

1941–42: Larry plays for the world-famous Trail Smoke Eaters.

1944–45: Larry is drafted into the Canadian Army during World War II and serves on two Alberta bases, playing high-level hockey to boost morale.

1946–48: King Kwong stars with the New York Rovers and receives the city's Key to Chinatown.

April 15, 1947: Jackie Robinson breaks Major League Baseball's color barrier with the Brooklyn Dodgers.

May 14, 1947: The Chinese Immigration Act is repealed, and Chinese Canadians are given the right to vote.

November 13, 1947: Japanese American Wat Misaka of the New York Knicks breaks the color barrier by becoming the first non-white player in the National Basketball Association (NBA).

March 13, 1948: Larry becomes the first player of Asian descent in the NHL.

August 21, 1948: Norman (Normie) Kwong suits up for his first professional football game with the Calgary Stampeders. Also nicknamed the China Clipper, he goes on to have a Hall of Fame career in Canadian football.

ALEXANDER CUP WINNERS
1950-51

1950–51: Larry wins the Most Valuable Player award in the Quebec Senior Hockey League. He leads the Valleyfield Braves to the Alexander Cup, the major senior championship of Canada.

1951–52: Larry battles Jean Béliveau for the goal-scoring lead in the Quebec Senior Hockey League.

1957–58: Larry scores 55 goals in 55 games for the Nottingham Panthers of the British National League.

January 18, 1958: Willie O'Ree becomes the NHL's first Black player.

1958–68: Larry becomes the first person of Asian descent to coach in a European senior hockey league. He coaches five Swiss teams over 10 years.

1964: Larry marries Audrey Craven.

1968: Larry's daughter, Kristina, is born.

Award and is inducted into the Okanagan Sports Hall of Fame, the BC Sports Hall of Fame and the Alberta Hockey Hall of Fame.

March 15, 2018: Larry dies in Calgary.

2021: The NHL pays tribute to Larry's hockey career and his historic achievement in breaking the color barrier as the first player of Asian descent in the league.

1972: Larry leaves his position as a tennis pro in Switzerland to own and manage Food-Vale supermarket in Calgary.

1979: Larry's wife, Audrey, dies.

1989: Larry marries Janine Boyer.

1996: Larry retires from the grocery business.

1999: Larry's wife, Janine, dies.

2010–16: Larry receives the BC Hockey Hall of Fame Pioneer

2022: The Government of Canada honors Larry and former NHL players Paul Jacobs, Henry Elmer "Buddy" Maracle, Fred Sasakamoose and Willie O'Ree for their key roles in "overcoming racial barriers in professional hockey." A bronze plaque in Toronto commemorates this "event of national historic significance."

Photos from the Larry Kwong Collection courtesy of Kristina Heintz

GLOSSARY

alien—a person who does not have citizenship rights in their country of residence

amateur—an athlete who is not paid to compete

Cantonese—a widely spoken Chinese language that originally came from southeastern China

Chinese Exclusion Act (United States)—a law that banned Chinese people from moving to America from 1882 to 1943

Chinese Immigration Act (Canada)—a Canadian law, also known as the Chinese Exclusion Act, that banned Chinese people from moving to Canada from 1923 to 1947

color barrier—a policy or unwritten rule to exclude non-white people

deported—legally forced out of a country

discrimination—unfair treatment of people based on their race, gender, beliefs or other characteristics

draft—compulsory enlistment in a country's armed forces

farm team—a minor-league team used by an NHL team to develop players

free agent—a player who is free to sign a contract with any team

Great Depression—an economic decline resulting in mass unemployment and poverty from 1929 to 1939

hat trick—the feat of scoring three goals in a game

immigration—the act of coming to live in a new country

junior—the hockey division for players up to age 21

juvenile—the hockey division Larry played in when he was 16 and 17

midget—the hockey division Larry played in when he was 14 and 15

Original Six—the six teams in the NHL from 1942 to 1967: Boston Bruins, Chicago Blackhawks, Detroit Red Wings, Montreal Canadiens, New York Rangers and Toronto Maple Leafs

player-coaches—sports-team members who both play and coach

professional—an athlete who is paid to compete

racism—negative attitudes toward or unfair treatment of people based on race

rep—short for "representative" and used to describe teams that represent a community or organization as one of the best in a specific age level

senior—the highest level of amateur hockey

shorthanded—having fewer players on the ice than the other team due to one or more penalties

smelter—a place where ore (rock containing metals) is melted to obtain the metal

stereotypes—commonly held but ignorant ideas about a whole group of people that sees them as all the same in certain ways

RESOURCES

PRINT

Fischler, Stan. *Behind the Net: 101 Incredible Hockey Stories.* Sports Publishing, 2013.

Johanson, Paula. *King Kwong: Larry Kwong, the China Clipper Who Broke the NHL Colour Barrier.* Doublejoy Books, 2020.

Ma, Adrian. *How the Chinese Created Canada.* Dragon Hill Publishing, 2010.

Mortillaro, Nicole. *Hockey Trailblazers.* Scholastic, 2012.

Reid, Ken. *One Night Only: Conversations with the NHL's One-Game Wonders.* ECW Press, 2016.

Wong, David H.T. *Escape to Gold Mountain: A Graphic History of the Chinese in North America.* Arsenal Pulp Press, 2012.

ONLINE

Asian American History 101: asianamericanhistory101.libsyn.com

BC Sports Hall of Fame: bcsportshall.com/honoured_member/larry-kwong

British Columbia Regional Digitized History: bcrdh.ca

The Canadian Encyclopedia: thecanadianencyclopedia.ca/article/larry-kwong

Multicultural History Society of Ontario: mhso.ca/tiesthatbind

The Museum & Archives of Vernon: vernonmuseum.ca/notable-citizens/larry-kwong

FILMS

Lost Years: A People's Struggle for Justice. Directed by Kenda Gee and Tom Radford. 2011.

The Shift: The Story of the China Clipper. Directed by Chester Sit and Wes Miron. 2013.

Links to external resources are for personal and/or educational use only and are provided in good faith without any express or implied warranty. There is no guarantee given as to the accuracy or currency of any individual item. The authors and publisher provide links as a service to readers. This does not imply any endorsement by the authors or publisher of any of the content accessed through these links.

ACKNOWLEDGMENTS

We acknowledge the Traditional Territory of the Syilx Okanagan People, where Larry Kwong grew up and where much of this book was written.

This book came together with the support of Larry and his family, who graciously shared their scrapbooks, albums and memories. We appreciate the witnesses to Larry's greatness who shared their impressions with us. Sincere thanks to those who sent statements about Larry's impact on the sport and on our society.

Cheers to the Vernon Museum and the historians documenting diverse stories. We appreciate the sportswriters in Larry's day and journalists like Tom Hawthorn who are keeping Larry's story in circulation. Hats off to Paula Johanson for her biography and to the other authors who have included Larry in their books. Kenda Gee and Chester Sit were close with Larry and produced extraordinary documentaries about his life. Gratitude to those who've brought Larry's story to TV, radio and the internet, and to everyone who's pushed for more recognition for our hero.

Special thanks to artist Amy Qi, to Troy Cunningham and Georgia Bradburne at Orca Book Publishers and to editor Kirstie Hudson for her encouragement, vision and guidance. Finally, thank you for reading. We know Larry would want you to go after your goals, just like he did.

—*Chad Soon and George Chiang*

INDEX

CHAD SOON is a fourth-generation Chinese Canadian. His parents encouraged him to do what he loved: draw, read and play hockey. Growing up on Vancouver Island, Chad dreamed of being an NHL star. He went as far as bantam house-league hockey before realizing that he wasn't going to be the next Larry Kwong. Chad now teaches in Larry Kwong's hometown of Vernon, British Columbia, where he realized another dream: writing this book.

KARIN BENEDICT

GEORGE CHIANG grew up loving and playing hockey in Etobicoke, Ontario. George is the composer of the internationally acclaimed musical Golden Lotus and the author of the children's books *The Railroad Adventures of Chen Sing* and *The Pioneer Adventures of Chen Sing*. He has directed and/or produced award-winning music videos for his songs, including *A World Away (Remix)* and *Old Montreal*, among others. George's acting credits include roles in *Eloise at the Plaza* and *McKenna Shoots for the Stars*. He lives in Stouffville, Ontario.

AMY QI is a Chinese Canadian illustrator with a passion for storytelling. A graduate of OCAD University, she loves to use vibrant colors to create whimsical and immersive illustrations. Her passion for art and storytelling comes from her love of video games and movies, both of which continue to inspire her to this day. Amy lives in Toronto.